A Short Course in Marriage

Moving from Frustration to Fulfillment

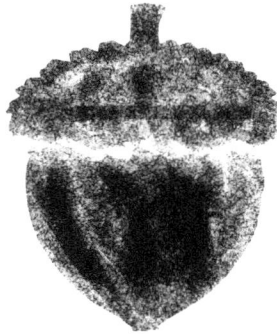

Edward B. Mitchell, D.Min., LMFT
Sharon L. Thompson, MA, LMFT

A Short Course in Marriage
Moving from Frustration to Fullfillment

©2016 by Edward B. Mitchell and Sharon L. Thompson

ISBN 978-0-578-18128-8

About This Book

This course contains the wisdom, experience, and skills of two marriage and family therapists with more than 50 years of professional experience between them. The focus of the content of this short course is on *what works*. Few thoughts are truly original. We, the authors, are grateful for the learnings we have gained from clients, teachers, writers and literature, ancient and new.

This course is designed for those couples who are committed to their marriage and wish to address their marriage from the level of tuning up to the level of major overhaul. If you are willing to expand your thinking and awareness about your marriage and willing to work for changes based on your contributions to your marital experience, this course can help you.

Table of Contents

About the Authors

Ed Mitchell has more than 45 years of experience as a marriage and family therapist and pastoral counselor. His Master of Divinity is from Princeton Theological Seminary, and his doctorate is from Louisville Presbyterian Seminary. His training was with many of the pioneers in the field of marriage and family therapy. Ed is presently semi-retired, serving as Director of Counseling at Bishop Simon Bruté College Seminary, affiliated with Marion University in Indianapolis.

Sharon Thompson brings to her professional career the analytic and constructive skills of a trained engineer (Purdue University) and the therapeutic skills of a marriage and family therapist (graduated magna cum laude). In addition, her work is grounded in theological training (Masters of Theological Studies from Anderson University School of Theology). She has a successful private practice seeing couples and individuals on the north side of Indianapolis.

Acknowledgements

We would like to thank Sue Pines for her wisdom and advice about publishing a book and for the helpful referrals to move our book forward. We would also like to thank Jennifer Lynn for her talents, patience, keen eye, and time she invested in the editing of this book. We also thank Aleata Halbig for her time, artistic talents, and the great job she did with the book's design and layout. These ladies helped make this a better book.

Preface

The writing of this book came about as a result of our desire to share the experience and wisdom that have resulted from our years as practicing marriage and family therapists. Finding a quality therapy experience for a troubled marriage can be a difficult process in and of itself. Consumers of counseling are often not in a good position to assess the skill and appropriateness of the therapy they receive. Couples seeking counseling are often at the mercy of the helpful intentions of others suggesting a counselor or may be faced with the difficult task of deciphering promotional websites which now abound and espouse the benefits of a practitioner's services.

This book is written in the hope that couples seeking help for their marriage will have a pragmatic guide to what has been found helpful to our clients over the years. Marital counseling can be both emotionally and financially expensive, and couples deserve clarity about what they can expect to receive from a counseling process. Of course the results of any such process depend on the honesty and willingness of the participants to do what is necessary to accomplish their goals. Therefore, it is important that clear goals be set and that their accomplishment be a measure of the value of the help they receive.

In these pages we hope you will find ideas and guidelines that will help you form appropriate expectations and intentions for the development and healing of your marital relationship. By no means does this book contain all the wisdom, skills, and tools necessary for the continuing task of healthy marital life. The intention in this writing is to be a pragmatic and encouraging guide to help marriages thrive.

We chose the acorn as a symbol and marker for our writing because we see it representing the "nutshells" of wisdom we hope to plant in your world and ours for the betterment and blessing of marriages and families. The acorn is a ubiquitous seed scattered through forests and neighborhoods; seeding new life, feeding present life, and promising to carry life on to future generations.

CHAPTER 1

Willingness

"We come to love not by finding a perfect person, but by learning to see an imperfect person perfectly."

—*Sam Keen*

"One advantage of marriage is that, when you fall out of love with him or he falls out of love with you, it keeps you together until you fall in again."

—*Judith Viorst*

In this chapter you will learn marriage is not about your spouse changing to make life happy and easier for you. Instead, you will learn that willingness to grow in self-awareness and maturity leads to deeper personal integrity and satisfaction. The more we know about ourselves, the better able we are to relate to another person.

The topic of love has always had a tendency toward magical thinking. From childhood stories like Cinderella to Hollywood movies, love seems to conquer all, no matter the adversity. While charming and even touching to our childlike hearts, grown-up loving is quite different. Committed love requires a willingness to grow, work, grieve, and take responsibility. Fairy tales most often leave out these things.

The Role of Willingness in Relationships

Most adults give intellectual assent to the proposition that adult loving involves work and responsibility. But too many adults don't see the need for their own personal growth and maturity for successful loving relationships. When push comes to shove, we tend to assume ourselves to be mature and insightful. We believe, with our childhood years behind, we have grown up. This belief is misleading.

Growing up, maturing, and gaining self-understanding are lifelong processes. Many choose not to participate in these processes and remain children in emotional and relational ways. These people can be hard to spot, *especially* when they are us. Such people may be professionally accomplished, financially successful, and hold positions of power in society. However, we would see these people very differently if we were married to

Nothing reveals our level of personal growth and maturity as clearly as participation in a long-term, intimate, committed relationship.

them. Nothing reveals our level of personal growth and maturity as clearly as participation in a long-term, intimate, committed relationship. This is where we really get naked, in ways we may not have expected. This is where we reveal and expose ourselves as perhaps no one else, even ourselves, has seen before. We cannot hide in marriage, and this is both a burden and a gift.

This is where willingness becomes crucial, willingness not only to work on a relationship, but also to grow in self-awareness and responsibility for who we are and how we act in an intimate relationship. A great temptation that erodes personal willingness is the desire to escape from this responsibility by focusing on the problems and developmental issues of our partner. Countless hours and dollars are wasted in marital therapy because a couple's primary motivation is proving the other to be at fault for their marital dysfunction. This approach never works and only brings greater pain and frustration. Blaming may be an attempt to achieve change without personal risk or effort, or it may be an attempt to avoid the pain and responsibility of self-awareness. Willingness, on the other hand, is the committed intention to both be open to doing something and giving the effort—mental, emotional, spiritual, and physical—to make change happen.

Willingness is clearly connected to commitment; for without commitment to bond and bind us in a relationship, we would more easily succumb to the temptation of blaming our partner and seeking out the next, "better" partner. Ask any experienced marital therapist, and they will tell you how common and unsuccessful this pattern is. The flaw in this mindset is revealed by the increased rate of divorce in second and third marriages. It is better to closely examine our own contribution to relationship problems to make the best choices about how to proceed. Without commitment, escape becomes a way of protecting us from the difficulties and pain of true self-awareness.

Willingness to take seriously our marital vows and accept the commitment to a deeper path of knowing and being known is part of God's plan for us. Since the time of Adam and Eve, it was deemed "not good" for the man (inclusive) to be alone, and so a partner was created. His partner was from the same flesh, but uniquely and wonderfully different. In this story the challenge and the blessing of life in partnership are born.

The story of Adam and Eve holds early clues to our desire to be "clueless." When something goes wrong we see, in the first story of man, the immediate attempts to avoid responsibility. Eve blames the snake, Adam blames Eve and then God for giving him the woman, and the snake slithers off having struck at the heel of our fear of exposure and responsibility. And so begins a history of hard-learned lessons.

Questions for Reflection

1. How committed do you believe yourself to be to work to improve your marriage?*

   0 --10

   Not at all   Absolutely committed

2. How committed do you see your partner to be to work to improve your marriage?

   0 --10

   Not at all   Absolutely committed

3. How committed does your partner see you to be to work to improve your marriage?**

          0 --10

    Not at all   Absolutely committed

(Save your answers and thoughts for when you have more confidence in your skill as a couple to discuss issues.)

* If your answer to #1 is 3 or below, ask yourself, "What will it take to increase my commitment to work on the relationship?"

** If your answer to #3 is 3 or below, ask yourself, "What would it take to increase my partner's assessment of my willingness to work on the relationship?"

The Problem with Willpower

Willingness is different from willpower in that willpower depends on individual determination and resources that often fall short or leave us feeling the weight of it all being on our shoulders. Willpower is rooted in a desire to control and have it our way. With willingness, there is openness to spiritual resources and the help and support of others, especially our spouse. These others encourage us in being and doing more than we might be able to do on our own.

Willingness is a cooperative venture with God and others that acknowledges the limits of our wisdom and ability. Willfulness, the cousin of willpower, is a desire to force our preferred outcome onto others and the world in which we live, believing we know what is best for ourselves and others.

Successful loving in marriage is not about willpower to do what must be done. Any one of us who has failed to keep a diet would be toast in a marriage if it came down to our ability to exercise our willpower to make it work. Willingness is not about control and forcing an outcome. Willingness is almost the opposite. It's about surrender. Surrender is an ego-disturbing term; it rubs us the wrong way. Our culture and our egos like words such as *victory*, *overcoming*, and *accomplishment*. But these concepts often depend on our willfulness to control ourselves and external factors, and in marriage that means controlling our partner. This doesn't tend to work too well. When we attempt to control another, we sow seeds of resentment that will become weeds in our marital garden.

To understand the inevitable reaction to our attempts to control, try this experiment. Ask your partner, child, or friend to hold out a hand, palm facing you, fingers pointed up. Don't tell them what you're up to; just ask them to try something with you. Then, take your own hand and slowly begin to push the other person's hand back. You will discover that most often the other person will automatically push back. It is an almost involuntary response, a basic instinct. Yet we try to push our partners and relationships, and we are often surprised and disappointed when they push back.

> *When we attempt to control another, we sow seeds of resentment that will become weeds in our marital garden.*

Surrender in a relationship between two healthy adults is a necessary ingredient for intimacy and more fulfilling love. It is not a sign of weakness—quite the contrary, it is an indication that one has a strong enough sense of self and well-being that they can allow another to influence them without being reactive. The basis of healthy surrender has its foundation in trust. Such trust has its strongest foundation in a faith in something larger than ourselves. For Christians this is belief in the loving nature of God as evidenced in the life and words of Jesus. Without such faith and trust, we tend to carry anxiety and vulnerability that lead us to believe we have to take care of ourselves against the harsh world, a threatening world that includes our partner. Such fear overburdens intimate relationships with the responsibilities of self-protection that can only lead to stress and mistrust. Relief from this anxiety will not be found in a marital relationship by itself but in the larger context of a healthy and trusting relationship with God.

Questions for Reflection

1. What is your belief about surrendering in an intimate relationship?

2. Identify three occasions where you have surrendered in your relationship.

3. Name three occasions where your partner has surrendered in your relationship.

4. How would you like to develop surrendering in your relationship?

The Power of Listening

Surrender depends on trust in something bigger than ourselves, bigger than our partner, and bigger than our marriage. It means allowing God and our partner to influence us, and to allow this we must listen, both to our partner and to our God. Without a listening relationship with God, our vulnerabilities and insecurities will once again seek to define reality, and this allows our fears and anxieties too much power. Learning to listen to God teaches us to have a loving, trusting relationship with our Creator and frames the context in which we relate to all others, including our marital partner.

Such listening to God has to be practiced and become a regular part of our daily experience. The challenges, vicissitudes, and threats of everyday life will drive us to defensiveness unless we experience a regular relationship with this power, which is able to bring us a sense of well-being in the face of all life presents to us. By *regular relationship,* we mean one that is practiced and developed on a daily basis, through prayer, reading, and quiet time, time when our own thoughts might recede enough to allow us to hear the influence of God in our lives.

Without a listening relationship with God, our vulnerabilities and insecurities will once again seek to define reality.

Held in the arms of God, we are better equipped to relate to life and to our partner. We have greater strength to look at who we really are, who we might become, and what is being asked of us in our relationship with God and with our partner.

Questions for Reflection

1. What helps you pay attention to your partner when they are talking to you?

2. What tells you your partner is or isn't listening to you?

3. What enables you to sense the presence and guidance of God in your life?

The Possibilities of Openness

Willingness is strongly related to openness. Openness is dependent on trust and the ability to risk. Partnership is a risk because it requires us to change and grow, to be self-aware and honest. Essentials for a successful and healthy relationship with a partner are found in the very nature of how God has created us. We can accept the way God has created us or we can refuse the deal and essentially become our own god, defining as best we can what life is about and how we will live it. For many of us, this has not worked well, despite our best intentions. Battered and brought to our knees, we have pleaded for a better way, one beyond our own ability to create. From our knees, we have found the basic truth that God is God; we are not. This is the beginning of wisdom and the ability to genuinely listen, to be genuinely willing to change, and to be willing to be willing.

Questions for Reflection

1. Identify a time when you have been most open to your partner.

2. What do you think allowed this openness?

3. When have you experienced your partner most open to you?

4. What do you think allowed their openness?

It is our willingness to be open, listening to ourselves and to our partner, which best prepares us for the growing and loving tasks of marriage.

CHAPTER 2

How It Works and How We're Made

"Love never ends. But as for prophecies, they will come to an end; as for tongues, they will cease; as for knowledge, it will come to an end. For we know only in part, and we prophesy only in part; but when the complete comes, the partial will come to an end. When I was a child, I spoke like a child, I thought like a child, I reasoned like a child; when I became an adult, I put an end to childish ways. For now we see in a mirror, dimly, but then we will see face to face. Now I know only in part; then I will know fully, even as I have been fully known."

—1 Cor 13:8–12 (ASV)

"You don't marry one person; you marry three: the person you think they are, the person they are, and the person they are going to become as a result of being married to you."

—Richard Needhan

There is something in the nature of committed relationship that eventually brings us to an opportunity for maturity and freedom that allows us to live our lives in a most generous and fulfilling way. The process that refines us to this level of living is one that requires a strong container, and that container is marriage. Within this container the compression, the grinding, and interaction of married life are similar to the activity in a chemist's mortar (the container) where the elements (persons) are bumped and blended together by the action of the pestle (intimate relationship). A reaction occurs and the elements begin to change, perhaps even purify, and a new substance, a new creation results. Such is marriage. This process appears to have distinct stages. Awareness of these stages allows us to be less reactive and more proactive in creating the marriage we desire.

In this chapter you will learn what the four stages of marriage are and what we experience in each stage. Each stage brings opportunity for growth, maturity, and deeper connection with our self, with our mate, and with God.

The Four Stages of Marriage

I. Idealization and Projection

II. Discovery and Disillusionment

III. Identity and Intimacy

IV. Love and Generativity

Stage I:
Idealization and Projection

"People are weird, when we find someone with weirdness that is compatible with our own, we team up and call it love."

—*Dr. Seuss*

"Marriage is a book of which the first chapter is written in poetry and the remaining chapters in prose."

—*Beverly Nichols*

In this section you will learn the dynamics that attract us to a partner and the hidden mysteries within this attraction that hold an unfolding adventure.

What brings people together in the first place and then leads them to make a commitment they really have no way of fully anticipating or understanding? At any stage in life, but especially in our young adulthood, we are searching for something, and that something often becomes someone. It is a natural part of life, the way we are created. Most of us do not seek to be alone; we actually long for a special connection with another person. When we encounter someone who seems to possess qualities we find attractive and desirable, we are drawn toward this person. If this person has a similar response to us, we have the right chemical formula for pursuing a relationship.

While we think we know the nature of our attractions to other people, in fact we are really basing our interests on minimal knowledge of who this other person really is and what our motivations really are. But it is on the basis of initial attraction that the process begins. In this stage we see others in their very best light; this is *idealization*. We tend to magnify the other person's positive attributes and minimize and ignore their deficits. We are drawn to a wonderful picture of the other person "Photoshopped" by our own desires. Naturally they respond quite well to being so idealized.

Simultaneously there is another process going on. All of us have deep within us, at an unconscious level, unhealed hurts, unmet needs, and greatest hopes for our relationship future. While we are focused on the perceived wonderful attributes of our partner, we are also attaching—*projecting*—a secret unexpressed contract that requires this other person to heal our wounds, meet our needs, and fulfill the hopes of our deepest relationship yearning. Quite an order, wouldn't you say?

> *We tend to magnify the other person's positive attributes and minimize and ignore their deficits.*

While this is a natural part of romantic union, it is also the sowing of the seeds of both trouble and a potential healing. In the bliss of idealization and the powerful yearnings of our projections, we feel we can do and be almost anything with our potential partner. And so a commitment is made and a journey of Homeric proportion begins.

Let us share the story of Tom and Sheri (the names have been changed to preserve confidentiality):

Tom and Sheri were a retired couple when they came to see Sharon. They had a shared Christian faith and trusted their pastor's recommendation for marriage counseling. Tom and Sheri were personable and likable. They sat next to each other on the couch, and both were open and engaging with each other and Sharon.

Sheri began by explaining her first husband died of a prolonged illness about five years earlier, and Tom's first wife died shortly after being diagnosed with cancer after many years of marriage. Sheri and Tom were friends, and Sheri helped care for Tom as he struggled with many health issues. Caregiving was a skill Sheri had honed during the latter part of her first marriage. They decided they should marry. Before they could celebrate their one-year anniversary, Sheri suggested talking to their pastor about John's angry mood and short temper. She could not understand his anger and wondered what she was doing wrong. She was aware that something was going on, and she was not willing to brush it to the side and pretend it was not there.

During therapy Tom realized that he was still grieving the loss of his first wife. Tom explained that they were best friends, and they had dreams for their future lives in their new home that they picked out and fixed up together. Sheri's personality and hobbies were quite different from those of Tom's first wife. Outside of both ladies being nurturing and good caregivers, little else lined up. Tom struggled with this more than either one of them expected.

Sheri projected onto Tom that he would remain the even-tempered, appreciative man she looked after while he was in the long-term care facility. Sheri also had old wounds of not being "enough," which this situation was reawakening in her. Tom projected onto Sheri not only that she would remove the pain of losing his best friend, but also that he expected those dreams of sharing that future to be fulfilled. The problem was that Sheri was not in those original dreams. Sheri was her own person and rightly so. Tom's reality could not live up to the projection. Neither one was getting their "wounds healed," at least not in the way they had hoped or expected.

Another example of how projection works comes from Ed's experience with a co-therapist with whom he worked for more than four years.

Ed was often grateful for this co-therapist's insights and ability when the group process was particularly difficult or challenging. It was good to know someone was competently in charge of the process. Toward the end of the first year of working together, Ed commented to his co-therapist that he was really glad she knew what was going on in the group that particular day. To his surprise, his co-therapist commented she thought he was the one who was in charge and leading the process that day. Both laughed and realized it had been helpful for each to project the aura of "knowing what to do" on the other when the group process was difficult.

The person we fall in love with is only seen at first through a veil, but in time will be seen face-to-face without idealized projections.

Questions for Reflection

1. What first attracted you to your partner?

2. What idealized characteristic of your partner has now faded that you really miss?

3. How do you think you may be different from your partner's initial perception of you?

Stage II: Discovery and Disillusionment

"...we also boast in our sufferings, knowing that suffering produces endurance, and endurance produces character, and character produces hope, and hope does not disappoint us..."

—Romans 5:3–5a (NRSV)

"You cannot start the next chapter of your life if you keep re-reading the last one."

—Anonymous

*In this section you will learn that the evolving difficulties
in our marriages lead us toward understanding ourselves
and the nature of loving relationship.*

As our projections and idealized pictures of our partner are
replaced by the time-exposing experience of who they really
are, a new stage of relationship begins. This is the stage of
Discovery and Disillusionment. It is here that our romantic
picture and experience of our partner erodes in the face of the
reality of sharing everyday life.

The partner who is revealed over time is made up of
both positive and negative characteristics. We discover good
things about our partners we didn't know. Attributes we found
attractive may well be sustained over time, but attributes we
ignored or were unaware of in the early stages of attraction
begin to intrude into our awareness. Some of these negative
attributes may have been hidden during the good behavior of
courtship; now, with familiarity, they slip into the longer-term
relationship.

If this were simply a matter of getting to know one
another, the adjustments of this stage would be less difficult
and conflictual. But there is a loss implicit in this process,
which can evoke a sense of betrayal. This new reality was not
the deal we bargained for. We married the person we knew in
Stage I, the stage of projection. Despite the vow we took "for
better or worse," we didn't expect this development, especially
not so soon. Add to this discovery the processes of leaving
home, financial responsibility, parenting, and keeping up with
whomever… there is a whole new life unfolding that, for most
of us, is unexpected and daunting.

Many of us responded to this development with a confident resolution to change… change our partner, that is. We remember that partner of Stage I, and we are determined to "assist" our partner in their return to being the wonderful person we knew in the first stage. The trouble is, that person never really existed.

The mission of trying to change another person is doomed to failure. It doesn't matter how convinced we are, even if a jury of our peers and family agrees with us, our picture of how another person should be will not be successfully imposed upon them. It just doesn't work. This fact does not stop partners from a lifelong drama of trying to change each other and resisting the other's efforts to bring about such change. Some people never get past this futile wrestling match.

…attributes we ignored or were unaware of in the early stages of attraction begin to intrude into our awareness.

Children and careers are often great distractions and replacement projects for frustrated husbands and wives who are unable to change each other. Examples of other distractions can include hobbies, television, work on or around the house, and sports. But in the case of children, husbands and wives may pursue co-parenting, throwing themselves into this project while neglecting the development of the marriage. While children may receive certain benefits from this arrangement, to their own deficit they may become too important to one or both parents and unconsciously absorb responsibility for their parents' well-being.

The over-responsible child, called the *hero,* can often appear as the model child, the perfect one who makes his or her parents proud. The rebellious child can be the one who brings shame to the family, seeming to find or make trouble at every turn. In reality both of these children live lives complicated by their parents' inability to meet each other's adult marital needs. The over-responsible child may appear successful, but too often their lives are built on pleasing others, a habit learned from needing to take care of the parents' emotional needs. These individuals often face an emptiness in later years, never having learned how to live the life that is determined by their own unique gifts, wants, and desires.

The opposite reaction of some children is to rebel, rejecting the role of being their parents' project and becoming instead "problem children" for the sake of their own identity's survival. The rebellious child pays a price for resisting servitude to their parents' defective marriage. This can be at the cost of personal, social, and sometimes legal negative consequences to their own lives. Ironically, this rebellious child's problems can provide a project which unites parents who otherwise lack common cause. Sometimes this roll is called the *scapegoat*, the one who provides the focus for what's "wrong" in the family. This is a sacrificial role in that the real problem lies with the parents' relationship but is bubbling out through the behavior of this child. However, if this rebel survives the risky behavior of being so oppositional,

...in the case of children, husbands and wives may pursue co-parenting, throwing themselves into this project while neglecting the development of the marriage.

in later life they might just have the freedom to live a life that is pleasing and fulfilling to themselves.

Other roles children may choose in the wake of dysfunctional marriages include the role of the *lost child,* the one who lays low and avoids the tension and conflict of the family. Such children are often quiet, don't cause trouble, and don't want to be noticed. They have a tendency to spend much time in their rooms. There is also the role of the *clown* or *entertainer,* who relieves the tension in the family through humor, often at their own expense. All of these roles are potentially interchangeable over time, but often because of the life scripts formed in early childhood, these roles can remain dominant into adulthood.

Marriages that overinvest in children and underinvest in the marriage make poor role models for children. They also make it difficult for children to leave home in a healthy manner. When children finally do leave home, a crisis can result for the parents as they face each other not knowing how to deal with their long-neglected relationship as husband and wife. Some await the future role of grandparenting; others drift apart, strangers to each other and not sure who they are, as a couple and as individuals. Good coupling requires a healthy sense of self.

A potential risk to relationships in Stage II is affairs. While there are many reasons for affairs, a primary motivator comes from the longing and desire for the powerful feelings experienced in Stage I. People in Stage II relationships sometimes decide they must have chosen the wrong person, because those wonderful feelings have gone. The person they knew in the beginning of their relationship seems to be gone, too. And so people, sometimes unaware, open themselves to the possibility of a new relationship where they can feel "special" again.

The problem, of course, is that a new relationship does not preclude the inevitable coming of Stage II. In every committed relationship, in time, the difficult waters of Stage II must be navigated. It is amazing how someone in their second "committed" relationship can decide, "I must have chosen the wrong person again," and then set off to find the next "right person." This may be why some people maintain prolonged affairs, never having to face the Stage II reality because of the lack of commitment and continued proximity of everyday life together. But it is these everyday realities that provide the opportunity for growth and maturity that comes with hanging in there as a committed and genuine partner.

Those who stay the course, for better or worse, and who are able to access the fondness of Stage I memories while struggling through the discoveries and disillusionment of Stage II, are rewarded by the richness of being able to accept loved ones as they are. This also allows the realization that we, too, are being loved and accepted as we are. This then presents the possibility and prospect of yet another stage of living in a committed relationship.

> *In every committed relationship, in time, the difficult waters of Stage II must be navigated.*

When we see and are seen face-to-face, a sense of loss will occur. It is here a new willingness to love must develop.

Questions for Reflection

1. What positive characteristics have been sustained in your marriage?

2. How do you think your partner would answer question #1?

3. What activities in your life may be distracting you from the attention needed for the health of your marriage?

Stage III:
Identity and Intimacy

"Why do you notice the small piece of dust that is in your friend's eye, but you don't notice the big piece of wood that is in your own?"

—Matt 7:3 (ERV)

"Everyone comes with baggage. Find someone who loves you enough to help you unpack."

—Anonymous

In this section you will learn the necessity and grace of self-examination that leads to compassion for ourselves and our partner. With new eyes we can see possibility and purpose in our relationship that we could not previously comprehend.

We are all flawed! No exceptions! Most of us get this intellectually and realize that not acknowledging this would appear as arrogance. But when it comes to the vulnerability of an intimate relationship, we too easily focus on the faults and shortcomings of our partner.

Deep down most of us have a fear of being abandoned or not being valued. The defensive part of our personality is developed to protect us from this. If we were truly known for whom we really are, we fear we would not be loved. In our attempts to avoid the pain of self-awareness, we seek to protect ourselves. We revert to basic strategies of fight or flight.

Only when we are authentically ourselves can we truly give ourselves to an intimate relationship. Becoming an authentic person is based on self-honesty and self-awareness.

Self-understanding and the ability to be close to another person are not well served by avoidance or by prosecuting the faults of our partner. Intimate relationships must begin with a deepening of self-understanding. Only when we are authentically ourselves can we truly give ourselves to an intimate relationship. Becoming an authentic person is based on self-honesty and self-awareness. A committed relationship creates the opportunity, even the necessity, for doing this work of self-understanding.

We don't know ourselves as well as we assume. As we continue to bump into the challenges of our relational life, we hopefully realize the futility of blaming others. If we can be honest enough to recognize repeated problem patterns in our relationship, and if we can be loving and trusting enough to explore our contribution to the problem, then we have reached a stage of growth and maturity that is integral to God's design for the healing and redeeming purpose of the intimate relationship.

It is here we must return to willingness, for it is willingness that allows us to face the daunting task of self-awareness. By self-awareness we mean a corrected picture of who we are, what we are seeking, how we defend ourselves, what we really want, and what we really fear. Fear is the dominant obstacle to self-awareness and intimacy. While fear has its place in the fabric of our defenses, most of us are burdened by too much fear, which then controls our thoughts, emotions, and behavior. Unfounded fear kills love. It seeks self-preservation no matter what. Too often what we fear are ghosts from the past and misperceptions of the present. And we forget what really matters. Fear can cause us to push away and even attack those we love, or to cling to another in a desperate and suffocating way.

> *Unfounded fear kills love.*

Fear, then, must be addressed if we are to push past the mine fields (or mind fields) of our defenses and learn who we are, how we love who we are, and how we share who we are with others. Surrender to an intimate relationship becomes not only more possible, but a fulfilling experience when we discover the gifts of self-acceptance based in a forgiveness and love that is bigger than our fear. This "something" beyond our own resources is a spiritual issue.

If we live in the conviction that we are alone in this world and our lives are under our control, we will not escape the damning influences of fear. Too often, life without belief in God becomes a path to cynicism, addiction, and despair. The God who made us continues to be involved in the unfolding process of our personal creation through which we become who we were made to be. With faith in our Creator, we can be encouraged to continue on, to "fear not," and experience the freedom of forgiveness that was the life-changing event of the woman at the well (John 4:1–42). The healing and freedom for this woman comes not through avoidance and deceit, but in being fully known for whom she was. In the light of this acceptance and being known, she was freed from her past and relieved of her need to hide. She goes to her village, where we might assume she was a figure held in contempt, but there she tells of this man she has met and how he knows her and has set her free. Perhaps a lesson for us here is that we are loved as we are and in this awareness we are ready to become who we are made to be.

The sticking points in our self-awareness and the problem spots in our intimate relationships are the doorways to self-knowledge and change.

The sticking points in our self-awareness and the problem spots in our intimate relationships are the doorways to self-knowledge and change. It is in focusing here, with honesty, both intellectual and emotional, that we discover who we are (see Chapter 4). When this is done with a partner in a committed relationship, this becomes the most intimate thing we will ever do, with the exception of our prayerful openness and submission to God.

It is not only the wholeness of the other we must come to love and accept, but our own broken and wonderful selves.

Questions for Reflection

1. How do you respond to disappointment in your relationship?

2. When do you feel most yourself, most at peace with yourself?

3. What spiritual practices are available to you, and are you using them?

Stage IV: Love and Generativity

"And now faith, hope, and love abide, these three; and the greatest of these is love."

—1 Cor 13:13 (NRSV)

"You will find as you look back upon your life, that the moments when you really lived are the moments when you have done things in the spirit of love."

—Henry Drummond

In this section you will learn that, freed from self-centered preoccupation, loving becomes a life-giving activity of new dimension.

Honesty and integrity slowly polish our souls in intimate relationship. Gems begin to evolve. Our ability to love, more deeply and more broadly, emerges in both a natural and, at the same time, miraculous way.

It should be no cause for shame that much of the first half of our lives is largely consumed by self-focus. This is a developmental reality. Even as husbands and wives and as parents, we are largely driven by ego. It is not that we don't love our partners. It is not that we don't love our children. But often these people are regarded as extensions of who we think we are. As such, we want them to be a particular way, one that reflects well on us and that meets our self-interest and emotional needs.

Freed from the task of relating in a self-defensive manner and the mission of creating a savior out of our partner, we are able to better love and accept ourselves and our partner.

In our Stage III process of Identity and Intimacy, we come to accept and embrace ourselves and our partners in a way that sets us free from the bondage of "perfecting" ourselves or our partners. We are free then to love ourselves and our partners in a much more unencumbered way. By *unencumbered* we mean not unduly influenced by the baggage of our past and the misguided belief that our personal resolution lies in the ministrations or submission of another person. We are conscious of these issues and do not need someone else to fix our past and make us whole.

Freed from the task of relating in a self-defensive manner and the mission of creating a savior out of our partner, we are able to better love and accept ourselves and our partner. Also we have new energy available to love and care for others, for the world and its people, in a non-neurotic way—non-neurotic in the sense that we are not seeking to see or change the world out of the need to resolve our own internal dilemmas. It is amazing how often some people's attempts to "help" others actually evidence an abusive and controlling character which tries to change and control another. In the end, who we are must be determined by our choices and the gifts given us by God.

With new energy we are able to become more powerfully co-creators with our Creator as we attune ourselves to the process of God's work here on Earth. People who care about others and this world become partners with the spirit of God working for the coming of His Kingdom. Language for this is not crucial; it is not limited to liberal or conservative vocabulary or theology. Intention and integrity of purpose are the essential elements of life lived fully in the spirit of Love and Generativity.

As we learn to love and accept ourselves and our partners, we are able to love others and the world with new energy and selflessness.

Questions for Reflection

1. Who have you known that lives in this stage, and what about them demonstrates this?

2. What signs of Stage IV do you see currently in your marriage?

3. What will bring your life more fully into Stage IV?

CHAPTER 3
Change Starts with You

"Fools have no interest in understanding; they only want to air their own opinions."

—Prov 18:2 (NLT)

"Affirm the value of change, and remember that it's a two-way street. The two of you are like mountain climbers, each lending a hand to the other, making suggestions and giving encouragement, as you work toward the same goal: a stronger, more fulfilling relationship."

—Jeanette and Robert Lauer

In this chapter you will learn more about changing your marriage. We have learned that forcing someone to heal our wounds and make us happy is not going to be productive or successful. Change takes self-examination, owning responsibility, listening, and realizing that we cannot do this alone.

Change in the marital relationship depends on each individual's willingness to take responsibility for their contributions to problems. It appears to be basic to our human nature to want someone else to take responsibility for the problems in our lives. This is a form of regressing to childhood when a parent or caretaker hopefully did what needed to be done to make our world okay.

Ed recently visited a family whose teenage daughter was still caught between being a regressed little girl and a more independent adolescent. As the afternoon progressed, this girl began to protest, "I'm hungry." This girl did nothing to avail herself to the food readily available in the house, and as it was not yet mealtime, no one was preparing food. Yet she persisted, in a whiny way, proclaiming her hunger like a little bird in a nest waiting to be fed.

It is important that all couples have a format that is helpful to them for discussing challenging issues.

This helpless and dependent strategy no longer continues to be effective as we become adults. Yet too often we stubbornly "hold our breath," place blame and, quite frankly, whine in order to change someone else so we will feel okay. It doesn't work, at least not in the long run.

The blessing and curse of adulthood is that we become the primary agents of change in our own lives, and with this comes the responsibility for whom and how we will be in our relationships. Here are some of the pitfalls we must avoid in order to be a healthy and responsible partner:

- **Blame is lame.** It is amazing how much energy people put into blaming others in order to address problems. This doesn't work! It at once puts the power for resolving the problem in another person's hands while at the same time irritating them with our complaints and unhappiness. This is not a formula for success. It reminds me of the futility of trying to teach a pig to sing. It doesn't work, and it greatly annoys the pig.

- **Codependence (being nice) doesn't work.** No matter how nice or compliant we try to be in a relationship, we have to be honest with ourselves and our partner regarding our experience and what we want. This is not about blaming; this is about telling the truth in a way that provides choice for us and our partners.

- **Tantrums don't work.** Regressing to primitive forms of anger is almost always destructive to trust and a sense of safety in a relationship. Tantrums give evidence to a lack of emotional intelligence and control of ourselves and only create drama and alienation.

- **Drama.** Drama has to do with various emotional interchanges that lead to no serious change in a relationship. Dramas are deceiving in that they appear in their intensity to have depth and meaning. But just like the dramas on television, these episodes are not real. They may be repeated frequently, but they do not bring about change. Emotional drama tends to be a way of avoiding responsibility for bringing about real change. It mistakes emotional expression for responsible behavior.

So what are we to do when we experience unhappiness or pain in our relationship and want it to be different? We must begin with self-examination. Ask yourself the following questions and reflect honestly on the answers:

- How important is this issue to me?

- How am I contributing to this problem?

- What am I willing to do to bring about a solution?

- What would a solution look like to me?

- What would a solution look like to my partner?

Exploring these questions through journaling, talking with a trusted friend (one not given to drama or side taking), or perhaps consulting with a counselor or pastor are first steps in responsibly addressing change in our relationship. Don't let your anxiousness to solve a problem move you too quickly into addressing your partner. The more clarity you can have before such dialogue, the better.

With this self-examination well explored, it is time to approach our partner. It is important that all couples have a format that is helpful to them for discussing challenging issues. This may have been something learned in premarital counseling, in a marriage class, or from reading a book. It is essential that each partner understand the rules that govern such conversation and agree to abide by these guidelines. We shall explore such tools in the next chapter.

One of the most essential ingredients of proactive loving in a committed relationship is our willingness to *listen*. This is a powerful gift that we have to offer our partner. Listening cannot be taken for granted, so when we want to have an important conversation, it is important that we accurately assess our partner's ability to listen to us at any given time. If either we or our partner are emotionally upset or stressed, it may be better to delay conversation until a calmer mood persists. And it is equally important that we be prepared to listen to our partner's response to what we have said. Often in important conversations we are so focused on what we want to communicate, we neglect this essential listening element of committed loving. So, even when we approach our partners with an important issue, we must hold space within ourselves that respects and listens to our partner's response, both verbally and nonverbally.

Remember, no matter what we request of our partner, our greatest power lies in what we do in addressing what is under our influence. This is one of the places where we are required to give well beyond 50 percent. We are required to give with the minds of those who trust in a loving and present God. We need to create a space within ourselves where we can tolerate frustrations and endure not knowing the outcome. This allows the development within us of a maturity and ability to cope with the rigors of life and relationship. It is okay to ask for help. We need to seek discernment, guidance, patience, timing, and strength.

> *...we must hold space within ourselves that respects and listens to our partner's response, both verbally and nonverbally.*

We must first put our own house in order. With acceptance and forgiveness of self, we discover the empathy to share life with another in a new way.

Questions for Reflection

1. Which of the pitfalls in this chapter do you need to address?

2. What allows for the best conversations with your partner?

3. What puts you in the best space to listen to your partner?

CHAPTER 4

Tools for a Healthy Self

"Then the eyes of both of them were opened, and they knew that they were naked; and then they sewed fig leaves together and made themselves loin coverings."

—Genesis 3:7

"Everything that irritates us about others can lead us to an understanding of ourselves."

—Carl G. Jung

In this chapter you will learn that the task of understanding ourselves is not a one-person job. There is much about ourselves that we do not know or resist knowing. Seeking the discerning insight of others, of God, and our own inner wisdom can help us grow a healthier self by bringing the unknown into awareness.

A healthy self is a necessary ingredient for healthy marriage. A healthy self is also a moving target. Age, circumstances, and culture all influence what it means to be a healthy person at any given time. There are, however, ways of measuring and evaluating ourselves that give us a better picture of who we really are and whom other people experience us to be.

Back in 1955, in the early days of self-help groups, two men, Joseph Luft and Harrington Ingram, developed a tool to help people better understand themselves. The tool is known as *Johari's Window,* shown below.

The Whole Me

I know. ------------------ **You know.**	**I don't know.** ------------------ **You know.**
I know. ------------------ **You don't know.**	**I don't know.** ------------------ **You don't know.**

As you can see, the tool is represented by four segments. These segments represent aspects of who we are that determine our experience and our functioning. Even self-awareness and the awareness of others do not complete the picture of who we are. Our own self-awareness includes only two of the four segments. The other two segments—what others know about us and we do not, and what neither we nor others know—make up a significant part of who we are. The relative size of each of these segments will change over time, hopefully with more of us being known by ourselves and others and less of us remaining unknown.

The first segment represents what is most obvious about us: known to us and to others. Some of this information is positive and favorable, some perhaps less favorable. But either way, it is a secret to no one and generally accepted as a part of who we are.

The second segment represents what others know about us but of which we remain unaware or refuse to acknowledge. This data is valuable to

...ways of measuring and evaluating ourselves ... give us a better picture of who we really are...

us if we want to better understand ourselves and increase our choices and how we can positively impact our relationships. These blind spots are not easily recognized even when others tell us about them. But in the context of trusting relationships, we can begin to learn more of who we are from honestly shared feedback from those who know us at many different levels—from partners, teachers, friends, and work associates. It should be noted that other people are not always objective in their feedback. Projections and manipulative motivations may influence the reporting of others. But this is why we seek out trusted friends and check such feedback with them to assess the accuracy. In our experience of doing couples groups, it has been interesting to observe a participant's surprise at hearing feedback from another group member that has already been given by their partner. This feedback is particularly impactful when it comes from a husband to another husband or a wife to another wife.

The third segment involves what we know about ourselves but others do not know. It is important to realize that we do have a right to privacy. AND, it is also said, "We are only as sick as our secrets." How do we reconcile these two seemingly disparate realities? We must use discretion regarding with whom we share private information. We need to have personal boundaries that provide us with a sense of safety and integrity. This is a healthy thing. At the same time, if we have a secret or secrets we keep only to ourselves, this often denotes the presence of shame and/or dishonesty, which will become toxic in us and our relationships over time. Having friends, counselors, pastors, and even a confessor with whom we can fully disclose is an important part of maintaining a healthy and whole self. Our spouse does not need to know every detail of our inner life as long as withholding of this information is not detrimental to our partner and our relationship. Discernment here can be aided by a trusted friend or mentor. You have a right to a private life, not a secret one.

The fourth segment is a part of ourselves we do not know and others do not know. This part is knowable, both through the tools and methods of psychology, relationship skills, and through spiritual practice. Psychological tools include reading, counseling, journaling, and group process. Relational tools involve honest and open dialogue with friends, "enemies," and committed partners. Why perceived enemies, you might ask? Sometimes we can learn the hard truth about ourselves from those who do not seek to protect us from what they see. While this can be painful, it can in fact be helpful.

You have a right to a private life, not a secret one.

In addition to Johari's Window, there are many tools from the world of counseling, life coaching, and spiritual direction that can help us better understand ourselves and develop a healthier self. These tools would include journaling, psychological testing, personality profiles, group and individual therapy, and a myriad of self-help books. In addition, there are spiritual tools that we can utilize, which include meditation, prayer, mindfulness, awareness exercises, holy reading, and seeking the presence of God. Psalm 139 tells us that God knows us before we are knit in our mother's womb. What a reminder that we are fully known and loved by the One who has brought us into being. Already known and loved by our Creator in all our aspects, we need not hide from knowing ourselves.

Tools are the means to behaviors that bring the love and life we desire.

Questions for Reflection

1. Who knows you best?

2. Do you have secrets that need to be addressed? With whom could you explore these?

3. What allows you or what would it take to be more gentle and accepting of yourself?

CHAPTER 5

Tools for a Healthy Relationship

"I can do all things through Christ which strengthens me."

—Phil 4:13 (KJV)

"Some people stay away from the door for the chance of it opening up."

—Billy Joel, "An Innocent Man"

In this chapter you will learn about tools that couples have found helpful as they maneuvered through some of the challenges experienced in marriage relationships.

Marriage is like a garden. It requires attention and regular effort. It must be watered, fertilized, and weeded. It requires sunshine and rich soil. There are many tools available to the gardening enthusiast that make his or her work more effective and less difficult. Tools also exist for those seeking to grow a healthy and vibrant marital garden.

Anyone who has planted a garden is aware of the effort required for success and, on the other hand, the malignant effects of neglect. A neglected marriage will choke on its own weeds. The joy of having a healthy garden and a healthy marriage comes only with a conscience tending to its needs. The next section describes some tools to nurture and grow a marriage.

Love's Many Forms

Michelle called, asking for an appointment for couple's counseling. She stated she and her husband, Tim, had not had a good marriage for several years. Michelle described it as, they were "living as roommates."

In their first session, Michelle described the event that resulted in a call for counseling. She had been looking forward to a date night that they had planned for several weeks. Michelle spent hours making dinner and creating a romantic setting with candles and soft music. The long anticipated evening arrived, and instead of Tim arriving with his own excitement, he called to inform Michelle he was going to be stuck at the office for several more hours. Michelle explained this was one hurt too many. She was willing to try marriage counseling as a last resort.

Michelle expressed that she felt taken for granted. Tim did not appreciate or even notice the effort she put into preparing a special night for them. Tim felt he could not please his wife. He explained that he had worked hard their entire marriage to provide Michelle with a nice house and expensive gifts. He felt she was not appreciative of his hard work and thoughtful gifts.

After both had the opportunity to express their frustrations, we began to talk about what made each of them feel loved. They began to understand that they had different "love languages." I directed them to The Five Love Languages website (www.5lovelanguages.com). I encouraged them to take the Love Language Quiz by Dr. Gary Chapman.

Discovering that "quality time" is what most effectively communicates love to Michelle was important information for both of them. It helped Michelle to understand why she felt so lonely and unloved when Tim would work late. It helped Tim understand his wife felt most loved by him and thus more emotionally connected with him when he spent one-on-one time with her. This meant more to her than the gifts in which he invested time (which took him away from the relationship) and money.

Each of us... has particular keys that unlock our hearts...

Tim began to take Michelle on dates. This created a situation where he could still feel good about spending money on her, but now it was happening in a way that really helped her to feel loved. It is not uncommon for men to experience love through appreciation of their efforts and physical touch. As Michelle began to feel more connected to Tim, she was more freely able to express her affection in terms of appreciation and physical touch. Together, Tim and Michelle began to explore how they could best express their love in the most effective ways.

Tim and Michelle had different "love languages." Dr. Chapman's book *The Five Love Languages* describes five ways to love and be shown love.* Dr. Chapman is a *New York Times* bestselling author, and this tool has helped couples identify and understand their own and their spouse's love languages since 1992. He believes that emotional love can be expressed and understood in these five languages:

Words of Affirmation

Quality Time

Receiving Gifts

Acts of Service

Physical Touch

While Gary Chapman identifies five predominant ways to express love, each of us, given our individual histories, has particular keys that unlock our hearts to receiving love. Discovering these portals requires self-understanding and exploration along with the courage to expose them to our partner.

Questions for Reflection

1. When in your life have you felt most loved?

2. How could you ask for that in your life right now?

3. What's at risk in asking for this?

The Benefits of Research

Jack and Diana came to marriage counseling looking for a way to better work through their arguments. Jack explained that the most recent argument they had was over making plans for their upcoming vacation. When they realized that they could not even plan a fun event without spiraling into an argument, they decided to seek help.

Jack was a lawyer and partner at his firm. Diana was an engineer at a large component company. Jack made decisions quickly and confidently. Diana also made decisions confidently but after careful considerations of many or most options.

They both argued their position skillfully, but to little avail. Jack insisted that he has been very successful in his career by making calculated decisions and moving forward. He and his clients were regularly satisfied with his choices. Jack wanted to book five-star hotels because they would provide the best service.

...among successful couples almost 70 percent of conflicts remain unresolved.

He would book the first flight he could find that would get them to their destination. He was confused and irritated when Diana would not agree with him. Diana did not always disagree with Jack's decisions, but she was frustrated and angry that he would not wait for her to do a little searching to see what was available and what their options were. Diana wanted to gather information and make a choice based on what offered the most benefits for the money. Diana insisted that she, too, made smart decisions and resented Jack for excluding her from the decision-making process. Diana interpreted this as his not valuing her opinion.

It was helpful for Jack and Diana to learn of the researcher John Gottman,* whose studies reveal that among successful couples almost 70 percent of conflicts remain unresolved. The lesson here is that problem solving is not always about coming to agreement but is more often (two out of three times) about learning to accept differences of opinion. For Jack and Diana, it normalized their experience of differences, and they felt less compelled to agree on everything. They also found it helpful to learn what Gottman identified as a needed balance of positive interactions to negative ones. Gottman's extensive research revealed what makes successful, happy marriage relationships and what leads to dissatisfied marriages or divorces. Gottman discovered the "five to one rule"—that is, couples who have five or more positive interactions for every negative one create the resilience for successful marriage. So for every negative comment or criticism, there needs to be at least five instances where a compliment or positive affirmation occurs. These compliments and affirmations need to be genuine but not necessarily monumental.

Before counseling, Jack and Diana had fallen into a cycle where anytime a decision had to be made, their defenses went up and they prepared to argue their point of view. As the conflict continued, Jack would begin to withdraw, emotionally and physically. When Diana sensed this, she pursued Jack with more energy to get him to reengage in the conversation. Jack had become "flooded." Flooding is another concept put forth by Gottman to describe what happens when our emotions determine our responses. This happens because our brains revert to more primitive response patterns when we become

---

*Dr. John Gottman has won numerous awards for his research on marital stability and divorce prediction. He is an author and professor and conducts marital workshops and training with his wife, Dr. Julie Schwartz Gottman.

emotionally overwhelmed, and our rational capacities are compromised. At such times when either partner recognizes that flooding has taken place, calling for a timeout can be most helpful.*

Jack and Diana agreed that their emotional energy would be better spent feeding their relationship instead of fighting to be right. It was helpful for them to consider the age-old question "Would you rather be right than happy?" They learned that it was acceptable to let Jack plan things his way some of the time and for Diana to plan events her way some of the time. Letting go of insisting on their own way became the loving thing to do for their relationship.

What's encouraging about this research is that no one is saying, "Don't argue." Arguments will happen in marriage. What research shows is that while we argue, we need to remember to affirm each other regularly, agree to disagree, and even find humor in our disagreements knowing that it is okay to be different people with different opinions and different personalities.

Questions for Reflection

1. What are your personal signs that you are flooding?

2. What do you recognize as your partner's indicators that they are flooding?

3. What damage control tools do you utilize?

*The timeout protocol can be found in the Appendix.

Stop, Listen, and Talk

John and Sue sought counseling because of John's concern about their sexual relationship. Sue felt pressured into coming to counseling and was not happy to be there. John initially dominated the session, expressing his exasperation about the loss of their physical intimacy.

Sue remained passive and unexpressive as John went on. When given the opportunity, Sue exclaimed that talking and counseling would do no good because John never listened and things never changed. It became clear that Sue was more angry than John had realized. She resented his verbal dominance and his attempts to control the relationship. The only way she knew how to make a stand for herself was to shut down, which included sexually.

Sue became interested when it was suggested to her and John that a communication tool which focused on listening might be helpful to their marriage. The Couple's Dialogue* is a tool developed by Harville Hendrix and Helen LaKelly Hunt that is designed to slow down the communication process and assure the opportunity for each person to be heard to their own satisfaction. As John and Sue began to use this tool, Sue became more confident that she could make a difference in the relationship as John began to pay attention to what mattered to her. John, for his part, learned that in the surrendering act of listening he helped to reestablish the connection he desired in the relationship, which eventually led to a more open and shared sexual relationship. It is interesting to note the parallel between communication and sex in their relationship.

*The Couple's Dialogue outline can be found in the Appendix.

**Sharing tools bring shared
discovery and blessings.**

Questions for Reflection

1. What impedes your ability to listen?

2. What, within your control, would allow you to listen more effectively?

3. What do you think your partner would most like to hear from you?

4. What would you most like to hear from your partner?

CHAPTER 6

Sex and Marriage

"For this reason a man will leave his father and mother and be united to his wife, and they will become one flesh. And the man and his wife were naked and felt no shame."

—Genesis 2:24-25 (NIV)

"Sex without love is as hollow and empty as love without sex."

—Hunter S. Thompson

In this chapter you will learn about the gift we have been given in sexuality. Our knowledge and underlying attitudes about sexuality greatly influence how we experience sex and how we participate in our sexual relationship with our partners.

Sex is the great gift, mystery, and conundrum of the marriage experience. In our many years as marital therapists, we have worked with countless couples regarding sexual issues. We've attended hundreds of hours of workshops, watching as the newest theories and techniques for sex therapy developed, refined, and sometimes evaporated. Opinions about sexual relationships is a shifting reality in the profession of marital therapy. New research and information, health issues, political influences, and moral/spiritual issues all influence what is always a very personal, powerful, and vulnerable part of who we are as individuals and as couples. Keeping in mind that this is a short course in marriage, and at the risk of great oversimplification, here are seven basic points to be taken seriously when addressing the sexual relationship:

Opinions about sexual relationships is a shifting reality in the profession of marital therapy.

1. Sex is best experienced within clear boundaries of marriage. This provides emotional, physical, and spiritual security.

2. Sex is best when there is a balance of giving and receiving for both partners. It is not for one partner to enjoy and the other partner to endure.

3. There is not one prescribed way for a couple to enjoy their sexual/erotic relationship. (There are, however, sexual behaviors that can put a marriage at risk, such as using sex as a reward or punishment, the use of pornography—together or individually—or regularly fantasizing about someone else while engaged with your partner [objectification].)

4. Personal limits and desires deserve respect. If someone does not want to engage in a specific behavior, they should not be shamed or manipulated into that behavior. However, sexual experimentation may be negotiated and provide new and healthy experiences.

5. Information about sexual functioning can be very helpful. Don't be afraid to seek out information about sexual health and functioning. Be aware sexual functioning can be affected by many variables, including emotional well-being, relational dynamics, health issues, and the aging process.

6. Every couple is different. Don't compare things like frequency. Don't look for "normal."

7. Mutual surrender is an essential element in the marital/sexual process, in which God refines us to grow in our ability to love and be loved as lovers. Learning to give to the other brings us rewards we may not have expected.

Healthy Sexuality in Marriage: Reclaiming the Gift

Sexuality in our culture has become a polarizing topic. Attitudes vary from an "anything goes" philosophy to sex being viewed as an uncomfortable and almost forbidden topic. This polarization can be seen in the Internet's pornographic portrayal of sexuality, on the one hand. On the other hand, we see the pervasive avoidance of parents when it comes to open and honest conversation with their children about sexuality.

Avoiding the discussion of sexuality with our children risks our forfeiting their formation as sexual beings to the ignorance and perversions of a culture that markets sex and people as commodities. Many of us remember "the conversation" we had with one of our parents. For many of us it was awkward and filled with tension, and a lot of attention was paid to what we should not do. For many of us it was not that helpful and set us up for finding our own way in this emotionally powerful area with its wonders and its risks.

> *Where sexuality has been repressed, we create a split that puts sexuality outside of our faith experience.*

In the book of Genesis we read that at the conclusion of creation, God refers to His Creation as "very good." This declaration of "very good" includes all of us and our God-given sexuality. How has this wonder-filled aspect of our created nature become so problematic? CS Lewis, in his book *Screwtape Letters*, creates a beautiful allegory suggesting how good and bad can get confused and turned upside down. In this story a senior devil named Screwtape coaches his junior devil nephew, Wormwood, in the ways of luring people away from God. Screwtape tells his nephew not to directly tempt people to do evil, knowing most people would be inclined to resist such temptation. Instead, Screwtape suggests designing temptations that deceive men and women into believing that they are doing good, when in fact they are not. Thus, people become confused and misled regarding the true nature of their thoughts and behavior. As a result, they end up taking pride in their goodness, while being duped into confusion and rejection of God's gifts.

Sexuality is a good example of how we can be confused and turned around, how something innately good can become something we fear and regard negatively. We are creatures made with sexual instincts, and this is not a mistake on God's part. But somehow we have become suspicious of this part of our nature. Perhaps this is in part because of the influence of an early Christian heresy called *Gnosticism* and its later manifestation, *Puritanism.* Gnosticism believed that only the spirit and soul are truly good and worthy of God's love and redemption. This split of body versus spirit is highly present in our culture today and ironically seduces us into a rejection of the God-given gift of our physical bodies and their functions.

> *Within the culture there is a propensity for using others, especially through objectification, and this leads to a loss of connection and isolation for all participants.*

If we do not address our sexuality in a helpful and healthy way, we end up deferring to the culture in which we live for our understanding of what sexuality is about. Our culture today too often defines sexuality under the strong influence of greed, lust, and the use of other people for selfish purposes. Sexuality is both a body and soul experience, a natural expression of our created nature and a hint toward the transcended nature of God's deep love for us. Sex is intended to be a pleasure that deepens intimacy. Unhealthy sexuality, while pursuing the pleasure of sex, too often leads to shame and alienation from others. Unhealthy sexuality frequently becomes more stagnant and boring with time, requiring increased intensity, such as multiple partners or hours on the computer seeking alluring and illusive satisfaction. This is not unlike the dynamics of addictive activities. Without connection and intimacy, there will never be enough. This is not what sexuality was meant to be. Within the nature of healthy sexuality, we learn something of the potential for relationship in fulfilling our deepest needs. The longing for our partner points to an eternal longing within us that beckons us toward our relationship with our creator.

Healthy sexuality for couples does require effort. We are called upon to strive every day to help our partner become more of who they can be, including their sexual selves. We are called to be willing to stretch our own comfort zone in our sexual relationship, without participating in behaviors that would feel violating to our spirit or body. Healthy sexuality requires an open communication and availability. Time and space must be created for both of these, remembering that our sexual relationship is part of our sacred bond of marriage. The couple celebrating the sacred mysteries of marital love should not be shy about enjoying all the senses as they set the stage for becoming one flesh (Eph 5:31).

In the mystery and power of our sexuality, intimate and intense sharing moves us beyond ourselves to transcendent oneness.

Questions for Reflection

1. What have been the greatest influences on your sexual beliefs and attitudes?

2. What aspect of your sexuality has been the most difficult to share with your partner?

3. What would you like to change about your sexual relationship with your partner?

CHAPTER 7

Money and Marriage

"A budget is telling your money where to go instead of wondering where it went."

—Dave Ramsey

"Bickering about money is the top source of friction among couples in the United States, trumping… kids, work, chores—even sex."

—Lynnette Khalfani-Cox (AARP)

In this chapter you will learn that our individual beliefs about money need to be discovered and discussed with each other. A list of questions is offered as a catalyst to explore your own thoughts and feelings about money, then this is to be shared with each other.

Money is one of the classic problem issues for married couples, along with sex, children, and in-laws. Money, like sex, is a powerful issue because money has a way of affecting our self-image and our sense of control.

It is amazing how one simple word puts stark fear into the hearts of many clients, and that word is… budget. Most people avoid this task more than taxes or funeral planning. Money is a complex issue, with many internalized rules, fears, and assumptions. Frequently individuals come to marriage with different convictions about money. Some are obvious and others are sometimes difficult to identify, but these always influence choices and behaviors.

For a couple to address money conflicts successfully, each person must first be willing to examine their own relationship to money. Here are some helpful questions for couples to explore individually and then share with each other before they attempt to resolve money conflicts.

1. How did my father deal with money?

2. How did my mother deal with money?

3. How does money affect my self-esteem?

4. What would my life be like if my financial resources were dramatically reduced? Increased?

5. What is my greatest fear about money?

6. What is my greatest hope about money?

7. How much money is enough?

Each partner should take time to write out answers to these questions. Then the answers can be shared with each other. It is important not to listen with a critical mind, but with openness to understanding what motivates and affects your partner when it comes to money. Having explored these issues together, you will be in a better place to address questions of money management in your marriage.

Examination and disclosure of attitudes, fears, and goals regarding money is necessary for sharing a healthy financial life in marriage.

CHAPTER 8
Addiction

"Can a man carry fire next to his chest and his clothes
not be burned?"

—Proverbs 6:27 (ESV)

"When there is no enemy within, the enemies outside
cannot hurt you."

—African proverb

---

*In this chapter you will learn there are many types of
addictions. Addictions will always take away from, not
add to, the marriage relationship. Addiction is "cunning,
baffling and powerful,"* but there is hope and help
available for all.*

---

*The Big Book of Alcoholics Anonymous

Addiction is a pervasive influence in our society today. Awareness of this problem is muted by our culture's normalization of addictive habits and our personal capacity for denial. But make no mistake about it, addiction in its many forms is taking a toll on countless individuals, marriages, and families every day. Addiction is the dysfunctional and destructive abuse of a substance, behavior, or relationship that brings about negative, even deadly, results for the addict and those who are related in any way to the addicted person. Most of us think of drugs and alcohol when we think about addiction, and indeed these addictions are epidemic in our culture. But many other forms of addiction exist. While most of us are aware of the extensive problem of obesity in our country, we seldom connect the dots and realize that most often this obesity is caused by a person's addictive relationship with food. Obesity is not just the failure of self-will; it is a biochemically and emotionally reinforced addiction.

Addiction is the dysfunctional and destructive abuse of a substance, behavior, or relationship that brings about negative, even deadly, results for the addict and those who are related in any way to the addicted person.

Most of us are at least vaguely aware of the extensive explosion of pornography use because of the Internet. The sex addict is not some lone and strange figure off in a far-distant corner of society spending inordinate amounts of time and money on Internet-related sexuality. The primary victims of this addiction are millions of good people, predominantly men but also women, who are unable to break the addictive dynamics with which the porn industry has, with calculated accuracy, trapped people who were "just curious." Even more distressing is the seducing of young people, children, by the purveyors of these perverse materials. Healthy sexuality is distorted through exposure to the exaggerations and perversions of pornography.

Help is available, but it must be sought.

Gambling is also an addictive problem in our country, destroying people's personal lives, financial lives, and family lives. Both online gambling providers and casinos understand the science of human behavior and use this knowledge to transform people from curious players to ruinously addicted victims.

Addiction is everywhere and takes many forms. Even a relationship can have an addictive pattern. We've all known someone who remained in a relationship, in the name of love, that was clearly destructive to them. *Codependency* is a term that applies to such relationships, where someone makes it their mission to "fix" another person's life, disregarding the cost to themselves. People in codependent relationships have not learned the truth that insanity is defined by doing the same thing over and over and expecting different results.

Addiction must be acknowledged before change can take place. This is not an easy matter for the addicted person or people close to that person because the primary psychological defense for addicts and those close to the addict is denial. Denial is amazing in its capacity to allow us to distort reality. Yet there are those in our lives who will see addictive problems and confront those involved. These people are saints, actually prophets in the biblical sense, who say the difficult thing in order to bring the lost into redemption.

Help is available, but it must be sought. Addiction cannot be defeated through individual effort. The wisdom of 12-step programs, grounded in spirituality, abounds in many communities. Such programs provide "experience, strength, and hope,"* and hope for those desiring to escape the grasp of addiction. Collateral 12-step programs exist for spouses, parents, children, and friends of the addicts who seek to escape the tyranny of addictive disease.

Addiction is not stronger than God, or as Betsy ten Boom put it, "There is no pit so deep that God is not deeper still." Yet one must be willing to do whatever it takes to genuinely arrest the destructive influence of addiction and claim the hope of new life available in recovery. As stated earlier, we seek the transcendent experience that can only be filled by our Creator.

Here are some of the recovery programs you can check out online:

- Alcoholics Anonymous: www.aa.org

- Al-Anon: www.al-anon.alateen.org

- Narcotics Anonymous: www.na.org

- Sex Addicts Anonymous: www.saa-recovery.org

- Sexaholics Anonymous: www.sa.org

- Sex and Love Addicts Anonymous: www.slaafws.org

- Overeaters Anonymous: www.oa.org

- Gamblers Anonymous: www.gamblersanonymous.org

*The Big Book of Alcoholics Anonymous

While it is a free gift, life is difficult. How we deal with our fears and anxieties is crucial to whether we die bit by bit or live and thrive.

Questions for Reflection

1. Have you and your partner explored each other's family histories of problems with addiction?

2. What conversation about addiction would you like to have with your partner?

3. Is there a behavior in your life that is or is on the verge of being addictive? Whom could you talk with about this concern who would be helpful? When would be the right time to share this concern with your partner?

CHAPTER 9
Safety

"Those who are kind reward themselves, but the cruel do themselves harm."

—Prov 11:17 (NRSVA)

"All marriages are sacred, but all are not safe."

—Rob Jackson

"The ache for home lives in all of us, the safe place where we can go as we are and not be questioned."

—Maya Angelou

In this chapter you will learn what abusive behavior looks like, how abuse can affect the one to whom it is directed, and how it affects those witnessing the behavior. It is harmful to everyone involved. You will also learn what you can do if you find yourself in an unsafe relationship.

Feeling safe is foundational in a marriage relationship. Our marriage should be a safe haven—the place we can go and be vulnerable, transparent, and honest knowing we will be treated with respect, compassion, and kindness. Marriage is a place where we can do our greatest growth, and this should be done in a safe atmosphere.

If there is abuse in your relationship, it must stop. While commitment is one of the foundations of marriage, commitment should not be an excuse for permitting abuse. This is not God's intention for us. If God's beloved—you—is being harmed by an abusive spouse, neither you nor your spouse can be wholly available for God to do his work in you and through you.

> *...commitment should not be an excuse for permitting abuse.*

What does abuse look like? Consider the following questions:

- Are you or your spouse physical during times of anger (shoving, grabbing, hitting, hitting walls, etc.)?

- Are you or your spouse a very jealous person?

- Do you or your spouse try to control how the other thinks, dresses, who they see, who they talk to, or how they spend their time?

- Do conversations quickly escalate into threats?

- Is your spouse sometimes afraid of you, or are you afraid of them?

- Do you "walk on eggshells" around your spouse trying not to "set him or her off"?

- Does your spouse hold rigid boundaries for everyone in the family, while lacking any realistic control over his or her own behavior?

- Do expectations tyrannize your relationship?

These are all warning signs of abuse. If you are in chronic fear, this is a big red flag.

Abuse can take different forms. Abuse is any behavior that is used to control another human being through the use of fear, humiliation, or verbal or physical assault. Emotional abuse includes actions such as verbal abuse, cursing, emotional withdrawal, neglect, and constant criticism. More subtle tactics include intimidation, manipulation, constant blaming, and refusal to ever be pleased. Emotional abuse wears away at the victim's self-confidence, self-worth, and trust in their own perceptions. It also wears away physical health. Abusive relationships are stressful situations. If we are under continual stress, our emotional and physical health are compromised.

If stress is constant and unrelieved, the body has little time to relax and recover. The continual release of stress hormones causes blood pressure to rise, breathing and heart rates to speed up, blood vessels to constrict, and muscles to tense up. The immune system is suppressed. Stress disorders such as high blood pressure, headaches, neck and back pain, and other digestive problems can result. Studies have found a link between high levels of stress hormones and various diseases such as cancer. This physical toll is no small matter.

A person may not recognize the serious situation they are in. If you are a fish swimming in abusive waters your whole life, it may be hard to understand this is not the water in which God wants you to swim. The abusive environment may not seem wrong. It may feel familiar if you were a victim or witnessed abuse growing up. It may feel familiar if most or all of your intimate relationships have included abuse. The longer one is exposed to an abusive environment, the more difficult it can be to acknowledge and address.

Removing yourself from potential harm is the wise and courageous thing to do.

When you find yourself with someone who uses abusive behavior, often fear, anxiety (walking on eggshells), and lack of self-worth follows. The natural instinct can be to try to be "good enough" to make the offender stop being abusive. Your willingness to change can do many things, but stopping the abuse is not one of them. The problem is internal to the abuser. Nothing external will change this behavior. It is rooted in emotional and spiritual brokenness. "Trying harder" does nothing more than deplete the energy of the one "trying." And trying to use the same reasoning over and over with an abusive person is not a rational thing to do. Actually, it is participation in the craziness. Yet, something must be done.

Separation may be necessary. Such separation is not intended to hurt your spouse, but to do what is necessary for safety. The message may be, "I love you too much to allow you to continue that destructive behavior toward me and our family. I do not feel safe with you any more and that must change."

If the abuse does not stop, you must make the change by making yourself safe. Begin by getting out of isolation—tell trusted friends or family members, get professional help, and/ or separate until the abuse is no longer an issue. Removing yourself from potential harm is the wise and courageous thing to do. In faithful wisdom David chose to flee from Saul, and Joseph kept Jesus safe by fleeing from Herod. If a confronted abuser will not seek help, the victim must take action as did David and Joseph. Keep yourself and your children safe.

Children witnessing constant conflict and violence are terrified by this, and it puts them at risk for long-term mental health and behavioral problems. Boys especially are more likely to be aggressive and engage in criminal behavior if they grow up with domestic violence.

Once an abusive spouse agrees to seek help, their efforts must be consistent and openly communicated. Real effort must be seen in action over time; talk is not enough. Much effort must be put into changing old, unhealthy behavior and the underlying wounds that cause it. Abuser–victim dynamics will take time and intentional effort to understand. Both the roles of abuser and victim need attention in order to bring about lasting change. The effect the abusive cycle has had must also be addressed and appropriate corrections and amends made.

We must stay aware of risks that preclude love's ability to overcome danger. We must choose healthy paths to love ourselves and others.

Questions for Reflection

1. If safety is a concern for you in your relationship, whom can you talk to about this?

2. If safety is an issue for your well-being, where is a safe place you could go if needed?

3. Is there anything that could be done in your relationship or your home that could increase your sense of safety?

CHAPTER 10

Joy of Marriage

"In a time when nothing is more certain than change, the commitment of two people to one another has become difficult and rare. Yet, by its scarcity, the beauty and value of this exchange have only been enhanced."

—Robert Sexton

"What a happy and holy fashion it is that those who love one another should rest on the same pillow."

—Nathaniel Hawthorne

In this chapter you will review the process by which marriage reveals to us who we are, not only in our personality but also in our created nature, and who we become through the rigors and blessing of intimate relationship.

As we reflect on the spirit of this book, we are aware of the challenge and hard work in marriage as we are presenting it. So the question becomes, "Why do this work—shouldn't it be easier?" It may be that a few are blessed with an easier path, but in our professional and personal experience we see that challenging and sometime difficult work is required to grow into the people God has created us to be. And it is our belief that "the crucible" of marriage provides a context and a reason to do this work. This context is the commitment we made, along with the private and cultural expectations to live out that marriage commitment. There is a desire to succeed in this important relationship. To end a marriage always represents a failure at some level, even when divorce may be the more healthy choice.

> *The core piece of who we are is that part of us that yearns for connection.*

This process has its joy and experiences of fulfillment and transforming love. Returning to the concept of the Stage I relationship, we remember the attraction and the wonder of experiencing what feels like pure love. While we addressed the elements of idealization and projection in the Stage I relationship, it is also important to consider the nascent elements of divine love experienced in these moments. Our creator does not tease and torment us with a taste of something that is forever unavailable to us. However, the greater rewards of loving come most fully through the process of maturing, growing, and learning that takes place as we recognize who we are. The core piece of who we are is that part of us that yearns for connection. While our egos, out of fear and selfishness, would love to believe we do not really need anyone else, this is a lie. We are created for relationship.

We were recently deeply moved by a video in a workshop on child development where a baby was deprived of her mother's facial response while she sat in front of her. The baby was initially confused and tried with increasing frustration to reengage her mother. It was painful to watch the level of distress experienced by this child. While maturity brings us to a place of learning to tolerate periods of limited connection with others, the need to interact, to be seen, and to be loved dwells deep inside each of us.

As we mature we learn to fully embrace all of who we are—our perceived strengths and weaknesses, and our need for connection. Simultaneously we are developing the capacity to accept love and to extend it to another, even as we see their strengths and weaknesses. Herein lies the gift of marriage and the reason for doing the work. We learn how to stay connected and offer connection, the foundation of what it means to love.

Such connection calls for us to fully face ourselves in a way that less intense relationships do not provoke. When someone knows us well and chooses to love us, despite their disappointments and unmet expectations, this creates an experience of acceptance that comes closer to the experience of God's love for us.

Recall for a moment an experience where you have loved and perhaps felt loved in an inexpressible way. Within that experience lays a taste of God's love for each of us. This is not an exaggeration; it is evidence of God's incarnate love that many of us long for in our depths. While it is stunning to conceive of God's love for us as only dimly experienced in our love for and from another, it is important to recognize this is the love He feels for all of His creation, and this means you and me. This Creator who sees the wonder and beauty in each of us does not hold on to the frailties, the sins, and the mistakes each of us has made. All love comes from God (1 John 4:7). In order to trust this love we must learn to believe in the preciousness God clearly sees in us. It is most significant that Jesus taught us to pray by calling God "Abba" (Daddy), exemplifying trust with abandonment in the face of an adoring father.

The blessing of Stage I is an experience of the power of love that motivates us to move in the direction of love. So how do we live up to God's kind of loving? We don't. We are not perfect. But we have been given a process that allows us to grow and develop in our ability to give and receive love. Stage II marriage is the tempering process whereby our humanness is exposed and forces us to a new understanding of what love is about.

The blessing of Stage II is companionship and partnering in life's experiences, responsibilities, and adventures (pleasures). A life shared offers companionship and partnering in the experiences of co-parenting, sexual intimacy, financial responsibility, and support in the face of fears (e.g. financial, health, vocational, parenting, coping with extended family).

The blessing of Stage III is the joy of being you and the ability to enjoy others as they are. To sustain a marriage we have to learn to forgive beyond our sense of right and wrong. We have to learn to value mercy over control and our sense of justice. This brings us into participation in the nature of God's mercy and brings a new confidence that we can trust God's love and forgiveness far more than our own efforts to hide our perceived faults. The more we learn to forgive, we more deeply realize the nature of God's forgiveness and love for us, and the more we realize God's forgiveness the more fully and freely we learn to forgive and love others.

Stage IV blessings are multiple. It is here that we discover the incredible mystery of how rewarding giving can be. When we focus on what we want, we sow seeds of fear, manipulation, and defensiveness. But when we focus more freely on what we have to offer others, our lives become rich beyond expectation. We always have something to give no matter what our situation. The impact we can have on our world should not be limited by our bank accounts, the number of lives we might touch, our leadership abilities, or our prominence in our communities. One grandchild, one adolescent struggling to read, one lonely neighbor, one hungry or suffering soul—it is here that the opportunity to live more fully awaits us. The simple thought of "doing the next right thing" can guide us as we allow ourselves to be aware, as individuals and couples, of the needs around us. In these actions we create blessings for others, for ourselves, and for our relationships. This is the unfailing wealth we can share in the elder years of our marriage.

For Reflection

We suggest that you begin keeping a gratitude journal recording the experiences you regard as blessings within your marriage. Keep this journal for at least 30 days and consider sharing entries with your partner. And consider offering thanksgiving in prayer for these blessings.

CONCLUSION

"We should be aware that brokenness is God's way for our lives."

—Watchman Nee

"The only way we'll last forever, is broken together."

—Mark Hall of Casting Crowns,
from the song "Broken Together"

It is our hope and belief that the wisdom and experience we share in this book will encourage your awareness that your marriage is designed to grow and bless you. It is not an easy task. It is not uncommon for any of us to lose our direction in our marriage when the problems of life and relationship collide with the unhealed wounds and fears of our past and present. But it is precisely at these difficult junctures of married life that new possibilities and redemptive experiences await us. By *redemptive* we mean that from what appears to be impasses in our relationships can come experiences that grow us and move us in new healing directions.

Our marriages are by their very nature an environment that demands we grow beyond ourselves and beyond what we may have imagined we could become. The commitments we make and the rewards along the way lead us to new levels of development and loving that are produced in the transforming crucible of marriage. Here we learn to forgive, accept, and become more fully what we are intended to be. It is the difficulty and the challenges of marriage that break down our defenses and old patterns, allowing us to become open and available to a better and more fulfilling way of relating. This commitment to be married forces us into a new way of seeing ourselves, our partners, and life itself. Marriage forces us past our own limited resources into a life open to power and love beyond ourselves

A final note in this short course in marriage is the importance of acknowledging the need for help beyond ourselves to achieve the success and fulfillment marriage can bring us. As individuals it serves us well to have friends, mentors, spiritual directors, and counselors who can help us stay honest and maintain perspective. It is also important as couples to have others who support us not only as individuals but also as a couple. This can take the form of family, friends, spiritual community, and other couples or individuals who believe in the benefits and goodness of marriage. We are made for relationship, and marriage is one form of relationship that gives us great opportunity and challenge to live fulfilling lives.

> *As couples it is helpful to have others who support us not only as individuals but also as a couple.*

We are not meant to be alone nor are we meant to relate to only one other person. Emotional, spiritual, and physical health is supported by positive relationships in our lives. The nature of love is that it is most rewarding in the giving. As we mature in our marriages, we are better enabled to love others and our whole world.

APPENDIX

The Couple's Dialogue

We recommend that you use this Couple's Dialogue tool when you want to be listened to and understood, when you are concerned about something and want to discuss it, and/or you want to discuss a subject that might be sensitive.

Before using this tool, take a moment to reflect on the following:

- Regular practice of this tool will lead to clear and effective communication.

- This tool trains you to listen accurately to what your partner is saying and to have empathy for your partner's feelings.

- Over time, with consistent use of this tool, you will build a deeper emotional connection with your partner.

Note: *It is best that neither participant be emotionally overwhelmed for this discussion.*

Adapted from *Getting the Love You Want: A Guide for Couples* by Harville Hendrix (New York, NY: Holt Paperbacks, 2001).

Beginning the Dialogue

SENDER: The SENDER is the partner who wants to send a message. The SENDER must take the initiative and say, "I would like to have a Couple's Dialogue. Is now a good time?"

RECEIVER: It is the RECEIVER's job to grant the request for a Couple's Dialogue as soon as possible. If the RECEIVER is available, the response should be similar to "I'm available now." If the RECEIVER is not immediately available, the response should offer a time so that the SENDER knows when he or she will be heard.

The Opening Statement

When ready to initiate the dialogue, the SENDER should use "I" statements. Examples include:

- "I feel _____."
- "I want _____."
- "What has been bothering me is _____."

Keep it short and use only a few sentences at a time. You will be able to add content as the process unfolds.

Mirror What You Heard

After the SENDER's opening statement, the RECEIVER should repeat what the SENDER said.

Note: Don't be too polite and let your partner say more than you can repeat. Even if it seems intrusive, interrupt when you

*can hold no more and restate what you have heard. Doing
so prevents the loss of shared information and creates a
manageable pace for effective communication.*

The RECEIVER should start with statements such as the
following:

- "If I heard you right, _____."
- "If I've gotten it right, you said _____."
- "What I heard you say is _____."

The RECEIVER should follow up with a statement such as
"Did I get it?" in order to determine whether what was heard is
accurate and to facilitate further dialogue.

If the SENDER'S answer is no, the SENDER should repeat
what was not heard accurately.

The RECEIVER should mirror again and ask, "Did I get
it?" (If necessary, repeat this process until the SENDER agrees
the RECEIVER got it right.)

The RECEIVER should then ask, "Is there more about
that?" Adding the "that" helps limit the conversation to one
topic. Further, phrasing the question as "Is there more?" is
more inviting than "Anything else?" and facilitates continued
dialogue.

The SENDER can then continue sending the message, and
the RECEIVER should continue mirroring what was heard
and asking "Is there more about that?" until the message is
complete. Ideally, this process is accomplished in two or three
rounds.

Summarize the Message

When the message is complete, the RECEIVER should summarize the SENDER's overall message. Lead with, "Let me see if I got all of that...." When the SENDER indicates that the overall message has been heard accurately, the RECEIVER should follow up with "Did I get it all?" and move to the validation step.

Validate the Shared Perspective

Validation does not mean agreeing. Validation is the RECEIVER saying that the SENDER's perspective is understood.

To validate the SENDER's perspective, the RECEIVER should respond with thoughtful statements such as:

- "You make sense because _____."
- "It makes sense to me, given that you _____."
- "I can see what you are saying _____."

The RECEIVER does not have to agree with the SENDER but must see the logic or truth of the SENDER'S experience. Check with the SENDER to see if you are accurate by asking, "Did I hear you correctly?"

If the SENDER can verify the accuracy of what the RECEIVER heard, the dialogue can move to the empathy step. If not, the SENDER should clarify and allow the RECEIVER to mirror accurately.

Empathize with Your Partner

Empathy is putting yourself in the other person's shoes in order to understand your partner's emotional experience.

The RECEIVER should offer statements such as:

- "I can imagine that you might be feeling _____."
- "I can see that you are feeling _____."

Then, the RECEIVER should check for accuracy by asking:

- "Is that what you are feeling?"
- "Did I get your feeling right?"

Note that feelings are stated in one word, like *angry*, *confused*, *sad*, *hurt*, *happy*, and so on. Using more than one word ("You feel that you don't want to....") is a thought, not a feeling.

If the SENDER shares other feelings, the RECEIVER should mirror back what was heard and ask, "Is there more about that feeling?" If there is more, continue sharing and mirroring until the SENDER says there is no more for now.

Reverse Roles

Once the RECEIVER has successfully moved through all three steps (summarize, validate, and empathize), the RECEIVER says, "I would like to respond now."

Now it's time to switch roles. The new SENDER may respond to the message that was heard or express feelings or thoughts from his or her own experience.

The Timeout Protocol

The timeout tool is an extremely effective tool to use for damage control and responsibly managing sensitive or difficult conversations between couples. The tool itself has existed in various forms in the development of the field of marriage counseling. This tool is essentially a stop-action intervention and is designed to arrest escalating emotions that could lead to unhelpful or hurtful consequences. In order for this tool to work, it is necessary that the couple makes a shared agreement that when one of them requests a timeout, the other partner will cooperate.

Either partner in the relationship can request a timeout. When either partner recognizes that his or her capacity for rational and constructive conversation has been compromised by his or her own emotional reactions, this person should request a timeout. The phrasing of the timeout request is important. The initiating partner should begin by stating, "I need a timeout,"—not, "You need a timeout."

After the timeout has begun, it becomes the responsibility of the individual who initiated the timeout to reengage with his or her partner within a reasonable time. Be sure to give yourself enough time to calm your emotional state and be reasonably certain that you're able to readdress the conversation without emotions dominating your thoughts and choices. Again, it's important to reengage within a reasonable amount of time; otherwise, your partner can feel abandoned. An hour is a reasonable minimum amount of time, with 24 hours being about the maximum.

If, after a 24-hour period, you do not trust your ability to address the issue without emotions negatively affecting your participation, be sure to let your partner know you are not ready to continue. Then the two of you should discuss together alternatives for proceeding with effective conversation. Alternatives may include asking for an additional timeout or having a conversation with a neutral friend to seek help with how to better address the issue (as opposed to seeking support for one's own point of view). In addition, it could be beneficial to seek the help of a clergyperson or professional counselor who can facilitate your conversation, but it is important to have consensus regarding professional help.

Here is a summary of the steps for a timeout:

One partner recognizes that he or she is becoming emotionally overwhelmed during a conversation with his or her partner.

The overwhelmed partner requests a timeout.

Given the couple's pre-agreement, the timeout request is granted and the conversation stops.

The requesting partner is then responsible for reinitiating conversation on the issue within 1 to 24 hours.

If the 24-hour period is exceeded, the couple then addresses alternatives for continued conversation regarding the issue. (Consider use of the Couple's Dialogue when re-addressing difficult issues.)

Recognizing one's need for a timeout demonstrates self-awareness and is a mature and caring step toward relationship building. The intention behind using timeouts should always be motivated by genuine concern for yourself and your partner. We all get emotionally flooded. Awareness of this and taking responsibility for our part in our relationship makes the timeout tool a valuable component of our relationship skills.

For More Information

We hope you have found the material in our book helpful. For additional information, including articles and videos, or to contact us, please visit our website:

www.ashortcourseinmarriage.com